# SO FRAGiLE ARE THE BEAUTIFUL THINGS

## HAIKU AND OTHER NATURE POETRY

### LUKE LEVI

YELLOW LEAF PRESS

# ACKNOWLEDGMENTS

Some of the poems in this book were first published in the following places:

*Humana Obscura* (Fall/Winter 2021 issue: "so fragile," "soft as a kiss," "how softly," "only one sound," and "like dripping candle wax" Spring/Summer 2021 issue: "December—" and "silence—" Spring/Summer 2022 issue: "how easily it goes" and "waxy oak leaves")

*Presence* (Issue 70 July 2021: "remembering fragments—")

*Akitsu Quarterly* (Winter 2021: "migrating birds—")

*Fireflies' Light* (Issue 25: "silent night," "owl at sunset" and "Frozen Leaf")

*Narrative Northeast* (Haiku Corner 9: "house finch," "in the shape of a scythe," "in a dark place," "fading world —," "a brown finch call…" "early spring—," "how lonely it is to be feared")

*Failed Haiku* (Issue 65: "the fly," "the joke ran flat" and "picking up fallen leaves")

*Cold Moon Journal* ("hummingbird its beak a black sword" and "bee dusted in pollen")

*LitStream Magazine* ("Sunday morning—," "one yellow leaf," "the red sunset" and "left behind for new growth")

*Wales Haiku Journal* (Spring 2021: "the dog is silent")

*Autumn Moon Haiku Journal* (Issue 4:2 Spring/Summer 2021: "full moon" and "crickets chirping")

*Trash Panda Haiku* (Summer 2021: "in the world of concrete" and Winter 2021: "air quality alert")

*Haiku Journal* (Issue #68: "upon the flower")

*The Tide Rises, The Tide Falls* ("like wrinkles")

The short Mag ("after the hard freeze")

carry the sun
in your pocket
    and in your heart
in shadow times
when the light falls apart

carry the sun
in your iris
    glow forth
in times of no stars
when sunlight plays hide

carry the sun
or the moon
    bright as any star
never forget all lights
even Mars has a scar

you are a poem
that doesn't end

a cloud dissolving
and reforming
endlessly

# A DEER THIS MORNING

Upon the green velvet of summer
a buck licked the last dewdrops of the sun,
twisted its long neck in silence,

like the morning sun that
fell from parting clouds,
and watched me from afar,

as if he could see through me,
as if I were the thin clouds
that the sunlight broke through.

so fragile
are the beautiful things
withered flowers


. . . . . . . . . . . . . . . . . .


soft as a kiss
rain patting
the window


. . . . . . . . . . . . . . . . . .


migrating birds—
every tree
looks like home

I'm trying
to become
like the wind

flowing with
ease and
with no goal

going with
the flow
of life

a wanderer
who ends up
at the unexpected

summer—
a butterfly clings
to its old home

this apple tree
bears no fruit
but I love its shade

what is past
left in
the wind

a memory
is ethereal
less than pollen

yet we cling
to it as if it's
a growing tree

euphoric—
a cardinal sings
atop the cedar tree

. . . . . . . . . . . . . . . . .

the sky flickers
as if the sun is unsure
of its mood

. . . . . . . . . . . . . . . . .

bee
dusted in pollen
flies from the redbud

I twist in all
directions.

I'm a vine
seeking
something
to hold onto.


. . . . . . . . . . . . . . . . .


softly the light
comes falling
into spring


. . . . . . . . . . . . . . . . .


dragonfly
gazing into the sky
so blue it is

# FRUITLESS TREE

the wind pulled off
the leaves of the apple tree
and sideways the leaves

went blowing in gusts
of cold air
and the shriveled leaves

yellowed and freckled
floated like dandelions
near weightless as the day felt

leaves crumbled on the grass
and the wind took them
to the cedar forest

where the smell of decay
was as inviting
as the circling wind

daylight fell slowly
as if autumn
would never end

as if the leaves
would halt in the sunlight
so that I could pluck them

like the fruit
that the apple tree
never bore

but today the tree bore
autumn in its leaves
and will for years more

struggling—
a sparrow flies
against the wind

. . . . . . . . . . . . . . . . .

summer rain
but the sun still
shines from afar

beams of light
color the falling rain
with the sun

. . . . . . . . . . . . . . . . .

it comes closer
every day to the hills…
spring sun

# NEARING WINTER'S END

This flimsy day stuck between
a gray film of curled clouds and gentle rain.

Under the drooping cedar trees
weighed down by tears of a sky
longing for a glimpse of sun,

a lonesome bird called seven times
and the cedar valley carried its call
in the cold wind and rain.

Such a day walks on quiet
deer hoofs that leave no trace.

The deer's presence only seen
for an instant, through the breath
that blows gray as the low clouds.

autumn—
rain on ice-lined windows
like dripping candle wax

. . . . . . . . . . . . . . . . .

living is a bird
gliding in the wind
without flapping its wings

. . . . . . . . . . . . . . . .

Sunday morning—
house finches sing
the litany in the live oak

. . . . . . . . . . . . . . . .

the sun never departs;
it shines from flowers
in times of darkness

ripe gold sun
near winter's last breath...
a short relief in this cold wind

.................

December—
cedar pollen rising
out of the hills like smoke

.................

the sky
like yesterday
getting brighter

my mind flips between
opposing beliefs so much
that I forget who I was yesterday

. . . . . . . . . . . . . . . . .

the dog is silent
but its bark still echoes
from the cedar valley

. . . . . . . . . . . . . . . . .

in bed I rest
while wind blows hard
in the cedar valley…
a calm speaks
even through strong wind

picking up fallen leaves
the wind returns
them to my eyes

*Cannon Beach, Oregon*

remembering
fragments—
a seashell shard
wedged into the sand
disappears in the sea foam

how softly
the rain falls
on the oak hills

. . . . . . . . . . . . . . . . .

long spindle of shadow
behind the sunflower

some paths to the light
stretch far to reach warmth

. . . . . . . . . . . . . . . . .

field of sleeping grass
is copper in the waning light
of winter

these are moon days
        slow days of silence
still my life hurries by
like I am dreaming
a long dream

laugh:
the show of life
closes soon


. . . . . . . . . . . . . . . . .


from the passion flowers
a bee floating
into summer


. . . . . . . . . . . . . . . .


alone—
the hooting owl
awaits a return call


. . . . . . . . . . . . . . . .


after light rain
white crape myrtle flowers
sparkle in the sun

like a summer dress
the poppy flower
ruffles in the wind

. . . . . . . . . . . . . . . . .

broken flower stem
petals blow away
one by one

. . . . . . . . . . . . . . . . .

dark clouds
tease rain
but only sunlight falls

# COLD FRONT FROM ROCKY MOUNTAINS

the sky carries a song
from mountains of snow

on cold fingers it flicks
the oak trees frozen in ice

it sounds of flapping wings
and turns the whining windmill

to tell us winter is here
through all its effort

there still is a calling bird
its breath bellows in a circle of

smoke that pulls my heart
closer to this once-dreary day

deep within myself
there is an eternal summer
even on overcast days

.................

old friends returning
from winter voyages...
flying cardinals

.................

little pink cloud
floating in the sky
refuses to break apart

a warm wind
blows the tree swing—
the sound of childhood


. . . . . . . . . . . . . . . . .


house finch
calm as the wind-swept cedar
splashes water on its wings


. . . . . . . . . . . . . . . . .


the fly
on the page
reads Camus too

## CIRCLING HAWK AFTER TEXAS STORM

the hawk
its belly like muddy snow
flew into beams of light
pouring down from parting clouds

clouds plumed silver and perfect
peaks so high and invisible

the hawk's belly flashed white
from below

alone on the hunt
a white arrow cutting through clouds

the shadow of a misshapen cross
expanding and shrinking from plain to high hill

(we wait for the wind's rush
or make our own wings)

sky blue as a shallow sea
the hawk flies with clouds
and spins in gold light

early spring—
oak trees budding
yellow as the sun


. . . . . . . . . . . . . . . . .


beside the dead bushes
a bluebonnet
blooms

letting go—
a leaf
leaving the tree
becomes the bed
for new life

even in silence
there is sound—
crickets chirping

cotton-white cloud
soaring across the sky,
how far have you travelled?

. . . . . . . . . . . . . . . .

how lonely it is to be feared
by cheerful birds—
hawk atop fencepost

. . . . . . . . . . . . . . . .

the joke ran flat
my strangeness is now akin
to a two-legged dog

in this chill
even the white fox shivers
        its nose peeking
        from the knee-deep snow

something is happening
you can feel it
        under the sun
        in the cold light
        of morning

the owl hoots
outside at 11 pm—
good morning, Owl!

. . . . . . . . . . . . . . . . .

the end of December
have I changed with the seasons
or am I evergreen?

. . . . . . . . . . . . . . . . .

cold night
cedar trees shiver
from autumn's breath

silence—
a white heron soars
over the cedar hills

..................

GRASS REBIRTH

the sleeping autumn grass
is more golden with decay

its rebirth once more
starts with a short slumber
so that beauty can live on

cold morning—
singing birds huddling
on the branches

. . . . . . . . . . . . . . . .

come quickly
the warmth of summer
is falling from the flowers

light tells time

blue sky days move fast
and light rain means much thought

(the sun makes fast the day
and rain slows time)

in this reflection we find
to make use of sunlight

and play and read poetry
on rain days with no rhyme

no leaf blowing—
the clouds halt
like sleeping whales

.................

bright yellow bug
resting on my shirt
now we rest together

I'd love to be the light
streaming down
from the sky,
soar like the
black birds,
light as air,
free and
alive.

. . . . . . . . . . . . . . . . .

everyone
is asleep but me…
my eyes long for stars

why are you swerving
in and out of traffic?
we will all see
the same sunset

.................

winter in Texas
but summer still clings
to the leaves

.................

peeking out from the bush
a red fox spots
the pigeon

.................

in one breath
a turkey vulture soars
over the cedar ridge

## SHOUT

The green hills
shout their songs.
Clouds stretch
in an endless
stream above
the trees, dissolving
and reforming
to no end.

lone coyote
journeys over the plains
in this quiet quarantine


. . . . . . . . . . . . . . . . .


owl hooting
as I try to sleep
music of the night


. . . . . . . . . . . . . . . .


gray sky—
flock of birds
twist in the wind


. . . . . . . . . . . . . . . .


the sun drinks
the last dewdrops
from a redbud leaf

what is left
of the jet plane:
a line of white clouds

. . . . . . . . . . . . . . . . .

cold morning—
hermit thrush echoes
in the valley

. . . . . . . . . . . . . . . . .

where the hog died last year…wildflowers

. . . . . . . . . . . . . . . . .

breathe:
the sky was once
called a limit

## VERBENA

beneath the shade
of the cedar forest
sunlight hides

until long threads of light
break through the sky
to point at the hills

in the opening forest
a flower stretching to the sun
glows bright and purple

like wrinkles
only the foam is left
of the sea

. . . . . . . . . . . . . . . . .

as the tide flows
back to the lighthouse
a starfish emerges

. . . . . . . . . . . . . . . . .

crickets chirping
below the silence
of the moon

## TWO BIRDS

a bluebird sings
atop an old cedar tree

its eyes search
the clouds for love

it breathes the wind
that flutters its tail

while another bluebird
soars in the sky

at last the two disappear
within the tree's heart

countless red trees
dotting the hills
in dark amber


. . . . . . . . . . . . . . . . .


nothing speaks within
my thoughts are clouds
moving above with the stars


. . . . . . . . . . . . . . . . .


the sun ignites
a golden field
of swaying grass


. . . . . . . . . . . . . . . . .


three vultures
descending from clouds—
gathering for lunch

## FLYING HIGHER

a vulture circles
and its shadow spins
on a golden field

black feathers aglow
in the sun and wings
spread out to glide
in the wind

a cloud obscures
the light and turns
the field grey

in the clouds
the black dots
climb higher
fading like a sunset

stray cats
gathering at night—
mischief meeting

. . . . . . . . . . . . . . . . .

cold today
warm tomorrow—
my changing disposition

. . . . . . . . . . . . . . . . .

fallen leaves left
behind for new growth—
memories

. . . . . . . . . . . . . . . . .

singing cardinal—
red feathers fluttering
in the wind

## ROOSTER

in childhood
the rooster crowed
during early morning

once disdained
the rooster crowing
eventually became a gift

its crowing
a song echoing
over the hills

its metallic black feathers
shining like metal in the sun
smooth as mirrored water

unproductive day
but good news:
the owl returns
to hoot for us

...................

still alive
upon waking—
another gift

the wind
sings through
waving leaves

. . . . . . . . . . . . . . . . .

softly
the owl flaps its wings
over the moonlit field

. . . . . . . . . . . . . . . . .

upon the flower
bumblebee high on pollen
burrows into spring

. . . . . . . . . . . . . . . . .

in silence
black storm clouds
break apart

# FLYING OFF

a hawk
awakened by my footsteps
flies above the cedar forest

even though I was going to
sit about like her

in the silence
and warmth of a lemon sun
the hawk flapped its wings

and the soft sound echoed
in the valley

as if there was
a wave crashing somewhere

stinky red bug
sleeping on my shirt—
smelly friend

. . . . . . . . . . . . . . . . .

hovering birds
in the wind—
floating world

. . . . . . . . . . . . . . . . .

two butterflies
twirling in the garden
one last dance for autumn

stillness tonight—
a lone cricket
chirps

..................

flowers must fall
to give rise to
stars of snow

sun of sweet fire
    tongue of light
floats from heaven
down openings within the cedar forest
    as if it's no miracle

miracle—
spring blooms
from bare trees


. . . . . . . . . . . . . . . . .


wildflowers in bloom
winter becomes a distant
memory


. . . . . . . . . . . . . . . . .


hope lives
on a spiderweb
shivering in a rainstorm


. . . . . . . . . . . . . . . . .


all day clouds grow
to become confused
for white mountains

today I listen
to nature's music
a singing goldfinch

. . . . . . . . . . . . . . . . .

little bird sitting
on the crown of an oak tree—
warm sun days

. . . . . . . . . . . . . . . . .

flies on my arms and knees
while reading in the sun:
buzzing friends

. . . . . . . . . . . . . . . . .

within dewdrops
on drooping leaves
the blue sky

life is flowing
despite my troubles
I am still thankful

..................

sun and moon—
stars forming
their own light

..................

after dreaming
of floating in the sunlight
a hooting owl wakes me

## PASSING AUTUMN

Autumn sings
through falling leaves.

An earth half green,
its musky-sweet smell now twists in spirals,

skipping itself across the Texas hills.
Soft as the clouds mingling low,

passing as quick as the gray fox
crossing the golden field of grass,

a swift wind rushes
through the cedar valley.

amidst the flowers
of summer
a butterfly is born


.................

a finch calls
in the valley
only an echo returns


.................

gray cloak shrouds the sky
like murky water
the other world hides

sleepy squirrel
its belly on the stone
sunning with closed eyes


. . . . . . . . . . . . . . . . .


two hummingbirds twirl
in a fairy-like dance
above the flowers


. . . . . . . . . . . . . . . .


still alive…
I am just visiting
earth for a short 100 years


. . . . . . . . . . . . . . . . .


another dream
about another girl
still looking for her

dog barking
to the full moon—
primordial habit


. . . . . . . . . . . . . . . . . .


an inkblot shadow
of the mountainous clouds
hovers across the hills


. . . . . . . . . . . . . . . . . .


80° Fahrenheit
on Christmas day...
Santa's wearing shorts

snow-heavy cedar tree
branches drooping near the ground
an opened flower

. . . . . . . . . . . . . . . . .

the day moon
in the cloudless sky
woke up early today

one yellow leaf
of a dead tree
hangs onto the past


. . . . . . . . . . . . . . . . .


a hawk flies low
searching for the spring sun
above the cedars


. . . . . . . . . . . . . . . . .


no wind tonight
only the sound of rain
dripping from leaves

stillness

    sky of light
    rains down in autumn

    long lines touching
    the green oak hills

    where is the sound?
    only a few vultures
    mingling with clouds

    the stillness will do

    an invisible day
    that only the heart
    can see

beads of water dripping
down frozen vines—
melting candle

. . . . . . . . . . . . . . . . .

like white brushstrokes
of paint strewn across the sky
coiled clouds

. . . . . . . . . . . . . . . . .

memories return…
like leaves blowing
against the tree trunk
the old must be left behind
for new growth

## WINDY COLD

a wind blew the cold away
now spring crawls near in a yellow sun
and the dead grass i mowed
flew on wings like little grasshoppers
jumping and jumping

a wind blew the cold away
now i remember the warmth
that went hiding for so long

and little finches come flying
in the warmth of the sun
like the children running with their dogs
singing and singing
the singsong of the cold's end

all there is to know
about life is seen in the
wilting flower

. . . . . . . . . . . . . . . . .

in the world of concrete
a roadrunner dashes
across the street

. . . . . . . . . . . . . . . . .

dawn—
the cedar valley hides
beneath dense fog

. . . . . . . . . . . . . . . . .

clouds remaining stagnant
as if in a dream
stillness

in the heart of verbena
summer enters
the soul

. . . . . . . . . . . . . . . . . .

life crawling
up from its long sleep—
wildflower hills

. . . . . . . . . . . . . . . . . .

the cardinal calls
across the field...

a return greeting!

shadow of a thought

cut through shadow
or the tree may topple

(sunlight is soul
and cold is moonlight)

look inside your heart
dream a brighter dream

(as thoughts come true
even in their wordless talk)

the cosmos is you and me
and dreams are made for free

upon the wet leaves
the summer sun
dripping

full moon
within the raindrop
falling from a leaf

rebirth—
once-frozen redbud
now colored purple


. . . . . . . . . . . . . . . . .


in the shape of a scythe
the day moon waits
for nightfall


. . . . . . . . . . . . . . . . .


after the hard freeze
the prickly pear
blooms in spring

fresh snow tracks—
remnants of the hiding
rabbit

. . . . . . . . . . . . . . . . .

below melting branches
sleeping squirrel dreams
of a warm summer rain

. . . . . . . . . . . . . . . . .

the white sky and hills
show no distinction today
both are one

four-nerve daisy
golden under the sun
awakens

. . . . . . . . . . . . . . . . .

both sun and moon
hanging in the sky
one must give

. . . . . . . . . . . . . . . . .

soundless day—
a lone white cloud
takes its time

little cloud of rain
goes it alone
apart from the storm


. . . . . . . . . . . . . . . . .


even nature knows beauty—
dragonfly flies back
to the same flower


. . . . . . . . . . . . . . . . .


the red sunset
welcomes early-rising bats
in droves

upon the flower
a bee clinging
to summer

how many times
have I longed for summer

and when summer arrived,
asked for less heat?

a dark veil
muffles the sun
still its light shines through


. . . . . . . . . . . . . . . . .


I don't know
where I'm going

neither does
the circling
black bird

but once
a fair wind arises
it's gone

feathers on the grass
a Cooper's hawk circling
in the clouds


. . . . . . . . . . . . . . . . . .


windy—
falling leaves soar
up today


. . . . . . . . . . . . . . . . . .


dead tree
so long for now—
acorns on the soil


. . . . . . . . . . . . . . . . . .


all along the field
grasshoppers jump
for me

high in the sky
the day moon
cannot wait for night

. . . . . . . . . . . . . . . . .

a flower
at the end of winter
still has color to give

. . . . . . . . . . . . . . . . .

how ignored beauty is!
wasp pollinating
the flowers

. . . . . . . . . . . . . . . . .

all yesterdays
no more than wind
fluttering bird feathers

## LIVE OAK LEAVES

I wonder what you call it
when you see the wind

pulling the oak tree branches,
the starchy leaves shining white

in the sun, like mirrors reflecting
the pale sky that looks almost white

near the horizon; maybe it's
a song you feel without thinking,

a chorus you never tire of
because the next note sung

from a happy finch
is unexpected, a fleeting

feeling you can't grasp,
that you can only feel

when you become the
whispering trees.

hummingbird
its beak a black sword
piercing the sky

. . . . . . . . . . . . . . . . .

growing older—
the clouds are moving
too fast

only one sound
wide black wings flapping
above the live oak


. . . . . . . . . . . . . . . . .


reaching for the sun
poppy flowers
in spring


. . . . . . . . . . . . . . . . .


goldfinch in the cedar
its feet holding onto
autumn

the sound of spring—
a Bachman's sparrow sings
on a cedar branch

..................

in the pond
a turtle enters
the moon

..................

the wind's color—
rose petals blowing
in the wind

without my glasses
someone waving at me—
a tree branch

. . . . . . . . . . . . . . . . .

already sunset—
now I know why
hummingbirds fly fast

. . . . . . . . . . . . . . . . .

painted dots
of red in winter...
three cardinals on white branches

a poet is always obscure
        is more related to flowers
        than the crowd
refusing to follow
pre-made morals
        and laws
        and norms
shed away the old
        live as a flower
        without following
        only living

the eyes of earth
blink on and off—
lightning

...................

which world is real?
clouds moving
on the pond's surface—
this floating world
oscillates from a duck

...................

life is a flower
spin around
and it has already wilted

## OLD SELF

forgetting my old self
I melt into the sun
and become a bird
knowing that to live
I must fly further

water droplets
kissing the daisy
spring shower

like rain
sunshine falls
on the green hills

autumn wind
blowing from every
direction

like the soul
the wind finds
its way home

## OVERCAST

In this murky sky of gray film
nothing is clear; even the
cawing crow questions if
his call will be answered.

When the crow stops
and listens it is the
silence of lightning crawling
closer from miles away.

A hum from somewhere,
like a bee flying by the ear.
Then another caw, caw,
and black wings flap and

disappear behind the oak tree.
Gone like the sun under the hills.
Silence takes over for the
finches; the endless song pauses.

A day like this is reflected
through silence.

eventually memory
turns to star dust
mixing with everything
that came before and after

. . . . . . . . . . . . . . . . .

another New Year...
the old years
so long ago

in the warm night
crickets chirp loudly
summer lullaby

. . . . . . . . . . . . . . . . .

Hope is illusive.
The hawk hunts
elsewhere
instead of
waiting.

. . . . . . . . . . . . . . . . .

like the sunset
the butterfly flies away
too fast

sometimes I'm a drifting shadow
floating over the days like in a dream
where everything looks and feels blurry
      incomplete
a tale neither sad nor happy

a life told quickly
with little attachment to anything

nighttime lightning
illuminates white clouds
like midnight fireworks

. . . . . . . . . . . . . . . . .

the sky shouts:
mockingbird
in the cypress tree

. . . . . . . . . . . . . . . . .

cold day—
even the gray clouds
frozen in stillness

evening calm—
the hummingbird
slows down

..................

moonlight
on oak leaves
darkness is not so dark

..................

like a leaf
in the wind
autumn falls

almost a blur
scavenger bird
in the blue sky

. . . . . . . . . . . . . . . . .

quiet night
even the singing crickets
are sleeping

. . . . . . . . . . . . . . . . .

soft as velvet
the first cool wind
of autumn

. . . . . . . . . . . . . . . . .

leaf by leaf
the tree loses
its clothes

wasp
busy as the bee
humming to a flower

.................

in silence
yellow leaves fall
one by one

.................

warm day in winter
even the sunset
burns the sky

how easily it goes—
yellow butterfly
in the wind

. . . . . . . . . . . . . . . . .

deepening sky—
the blue growing darker and darker
as autumn nears

. . . . . . . . . . . . . . . . .

silence
colored white
falls from the sky

summer lets go
of its old self
fallen leaves

. . . . . . . . . . . . . . . . .

lonesome—
lizard hides
in the spoon yucca's shade

. . . . . . . . . . . . . . . . .

on my shirt
a resting bee
tired from work

. . . . . . . . . . . . . . . . .

with each new year
another wrinkle
to show the soul's depth

# MOONLIGHT

Fall your light on me, moon,
spread your light
across the green hills
like the stars above,
shimmering, blinking,
turning like leaves
in the wind.

summer's end
distilled to its essence
wilting sunflower


. . . . . . . . . . . . . . . . .


not so alone—
crickets sing louder
the warmer it gets


. . . . . . . . . . . . . . . . .


a butterfly
flies off with
the sunset's color

snail
drags its bed
up a brick wall

. . . . . . . . . . . . . . . . . .

spilled red paint
can become a sunset

even though you wanted
a blue sky

no one knows it was a mistake
and that mistake becomes art

my trade

my trade
is living
like a flower

to be one
with everything

then fall away
and return
to the universe

December—
red flowers
charred black

. . . . . . . . . . . . . . . . .

dragonfly
atop the flower
quiet as a cloud

. . . . . . . . . . . . . . . .

autumn wind—
pulling off its cloak
of leaves

have I always been alone
   like this hooting owl
   atop the house roof
   looking at the starry night?

or am I one of the stars
that appear so close together
   as if they are one?

sometimes my life
twists over too
leaf on the grass

. . . . . . . . . . . . . . . . . .

autumn—
an apple tree leaf
falls on my head

singing cardinal—
I am happy too
on this fall day

.................

live oak leaves
smooth as a still pond
after the flood

.................

golden light
in the morning
falls from a pale sky

## LINGERING CLOUD

Today there is no sound.
Clouds travel like fog,
taking their time,

just like the rabbit
who is hiding in the
middle of the garden.

That rascal!
But how can I complain
on a day like this?

I must meet the day
in case it flies away too fast.
Come, lingering cloud,

carry me over the hills with you.
Let us forget everything
and soar through the day.

air quality alert
the hawk in the clouds
doesn't know

. . . . . . . . . . . . . . . . .

calm as light rain
the morning sun
on white oak leaves

. . . . . . . . . . . . . . . .

a white pearl
floating on the pond
autumn moon

autumn—
a peach tree leaf
dances on the grass

. . . . . . . . . . . . . . . . . .

the sky like blue
window shutters

if only I could open them
to reach the other side

finding its way
across the Columbia River
a long line of sunlight

..................

sunny autumn—
shadows of cedar branches
sway on the ground

..................

lightning—
sometimes my heart
is erratic as this storm

autumn—
breaking into the clouds
a black bird


. . . . . . . . . . . . . . . . .


fallen leaves
scrape against gravel
blowing away the past


. . . . . . . . . . . . . . . .


dragonfly
near-invisible and motionless
meditating on a flower

## TWO SOUNDS

finches sang this morning
now thunder rumbles
like an angry lion

both sound harmonious
the comfort of light and dark

the sky full of night lightning
or a blinding sun

and both pull my heart
to listen for a moment
to feel something in each song

the hard thunder
and the soft call of the goldfinch

hills in shadow
hurricane clouds
stole the sunshine

. . . . . . . . . . . . . . . . . .

autumn—
a soaring black bird
free as the sky

. . . . . . . . . . . . . . . . .

deer in wildflower field...
how often the fragile things
are trampled on

. . . . . . . . . . . . . . . . .

she is beautiful
without her clothes
leafless tree

oak tree
a crescent of leaves
its legs pressed into the world

. . . . . . . . . . . . . . . . .

sinking into autumn
yellow leaves
in the pond

. . . . . . . . . . . . . . . . .

friend?
yellow finch
facing the bird statue

warm sun
the finch's tail
in the water

. . . . . . . . . . . . . . . . . .

dragonfly
on the Buddha
watching bees return

. . . . . . . . . . . . . . . . . .

stay still, heart,
as still as the dragonfly
disguised as a blue flower

# EARLY AUTUMN

light as air
a bee bumbles
into a flower

and the pink flower
shaped like a trumpet
falls into autumn

the bee tastes summer
one final time before
it sets off yet again

flying over
the next hill
like the morning mist

that hid the green hills
clouding the path
to the light

## THUNDER ABOVE THE FLOWERS

I feel at home
in the flowers,
even in raindrops
and in the dark clouds
that roar in hunger.

. . . . . . . . . . . . . . . . .

no moon reflected
but the pond
is full of stars

. . . . . . . . . . . . . . . . .

the lightest blue sky
singing birds will soon
fill the air with chatter

like a leaf falling
the butterfly travels
lightly

. . . . . . . . . . . . . . . .

fall migration—
a cawing bird
to say it's still here

. . . . . . . . . . . . . . . .

almost a whisper
the wings of the
butterfly

tears from the sky
in a pool of water
full of clouds


...................


the sky cried
for the singing birds
flew south


...................


even the flowers
that took their time
bloom

if I were a cloud
I'd fall as rain

then swim with fish
in rivers clear as
a shallow sea

jump from great
waterfalls to become
the ocean

then rise up again
as a cloud
and do it all again

Halloween—
pretending
to be dead

. . . . . . . . . . . . . . . . . .

caught
between two worlds
owl at sunset

. . . . . . . . . . . . . . . . . .

autumn—
an old windmill
cawing with a crow

its daily walk
is taking forever
caterpillar

. . . . . . . . . . . . . . . . .

after living like a monk
a possible romance
cottonmouth

. . . . . . . . . . . . . . . . .

on the drive home
the stars hang low
almost touching the hills

two finches separate—
going it alone
again

. . . . . . . . . . . . . . . . .

in a world of one color
a cardinal sings
on a snowy branch

. . . . . . . . . . . . . . . . .

Have I changed enough?
Am I better now?
New Year

out of silence an owl hoots twice…
the valley pulls its cry
in the wind

. . . . . . . . . . . . . . . . .

like this leaf
floating on the stream
I'll pass on

half the sky
shined pale blue
half a gray shroud
but no rain fell that day...
sunlight doused
the storm

.................

lingering autumn—
a butterfly catches the sun
in its wings

.................

delicate as sunlight
crumbling into earth
fallen maple leaf

# OLD FISHING MEMORY

I sat near a willow tree
that stretched to almost touch
the shady water on the far side
of the mountain stream.

There were dozens of fish
all huddled together,
as if to keep warm
in the cold stream.

A tail splashed the water
when my toes reached
the pebbles at the bottom,
and some of the fish scattered.

The fish swam to the shade
of the willow tree.
Slippery skins grazing me,
swimming in comfort.

Like they were a part of me
and I was there but not really,
not a person or anything defined,
just present.

The presence in the willow tree,
the water lapping against boulders,
the strange smell of coldness
that cracks the lips and makes the mouth dry.

A feeling of something
rise from the throat, choking in love,
like tears dripping from the snowy alders
to become the river, the sky, the world.

one bee
remains in autumn
drinking sun-kissed flowers

. . . . . . . . . . . . . . . . . .

I am always
in search of
forgotten flowers
in this floating world.
If you forget yourself,
everything can be a
flower that was
never seen
before.

autumn—
an owl hooting
in the screeching wind

. . . . . . . . . . . . . . . . .

maps in the sky
lines of long journeys
crisscross

. . . . . . . . . . . . . . . . .

falling one moment
then it's in flight...
autumn leaf

This morning birdsong
outside my window that awoke me
from deep within starry dreams
is like the light trickling in to fill
me with a heartfelt joy
despite my want to sleep
a little more.

wordless…
today is as silent
as the coming winter

...................

it shivers so much
that it has lost its leaves
peach tree

a splinter of light
    pokes through the clouds
finds its way
    across dark space
to become
    trees
    flowers
    the world

my blood is sunlight
    in the stillness
    of winter

autumn—
an owl hoots
near scraping branches

. . . . . . . . . . . . . . . . .

turning over
the fallen rose petal
autumn wind

. . . . . . . . . . . . . . . . .

morning fog
escapes the oak valley
silent as autumn

mistaken
for a butterfly
falling red leaf

. . . . . . . . . . . . . . . . . .

trying to be who I am
autumn drops
its old leaves

searching
for the adrift
    like the flashing beam
    of a lighthouse
a soaring hawk

it's dizzying
watching finches play
in this autumn sky

. . . . . . . . . . . . . . . . .

autumn—
a withered tree
claws at the sky

. . . . . . . . . . . . . . . . .

silent night—
a thin cloud passes
through the moon

white grass
solid as oak trees
frozen in silence

. . . . . . . . . . . . . . . . .

the day moon
keeps climbing up
a bare branch

# IN THE CRAPE MYRTLE

The cardinals, bright red birds
here in the Texas Hill Country,
were all male, wearing those red mohawks.

And their songs, which
are short and barely heard,
the wind carried,

along with the faint light
that broke through the sky.

When the sky opened
the sun shined on green hills,

and the cardinals, near glowing,
flew off in the light,
disappearing over the oak hills.

waxy oak leaves
shine white in the sun
flickering like stars

. . . . . . . . . . . . . . . . .

on the pond
cedar trees sway
in the ripples

. . . . . . . . . . . . . . . . .

in the ditch of life
nowhere to go but up…
blinking stars

Sometimes I feel so much
beauty in things,

small things
that are fragile
and infinite,

like the blue sky
or clouds or flowers,

that I can't breathe,
that I am no longer
one thing but many,

like the stars
in the universe.

heavy fog—
the tree I normally see
is a phantom

. . . . . . . . . . . . . . . . .

some things
are sweet to find
strawberries powdered in snow

. . . . . . . . . . . . . . . . .

on an April sky—
the color of the sea—
clouds embrace the sun

great change
is happening
    in the sky
    full of light
even the birds see it
    stretching far
    to the horizon
everything is breaking free
    even the light
    cutting through clouds

an owl on a branch
far into silence
hoot hoot


. . . . . . . . . . . . . . . . .


so tall on the pond
in the fading light
live oak tree


. . . . . . . . . . . . . . . . .


at the crown of a bare tree
a puffy bird
hanging with the day moon

## THE MIRROR

some days I'm asleep
some days I'm awake

drifting in and out of
lucid thoughts and
numbness

being who I am
and sometimes not…
maybe both days
I am still who I am:
sometimes wide awake
sometimes drifting in a dream

swoosh
of a brown hawk's wings
songbirds silent


. . . . . . . . . . . . . . . . .


warm yellow sun
but faraway clouds
foretell snow


. . . . . . . . . . . . . . . . .


wings outstretched
feet dripping of pond
blue heron


. . . . . . . . . . . . . . . . .


an owl hoots under a red moon…
its craters so close
you can lay in them

## FROZEN LEAF

Green
leaf
molded
in clear ice
waits for warmth to free
it from the cold's frozen embrace.

fading world—
shadows of the hills
during sunset

. . . . . . . . . . . . . . . . .

a brown finch call...
from the opposing cedar hill
a return greeting

prickly pear—
its scars and age
in black spots


..................


like opening flowers
outspread branches
of ice-lined cedar trees


..................


day moon—
brown hawk dives
like a jet plane

## UNSEEN

there is a strange
feeling in the wind
when it blows
in strong gusts

lifting up
leaves in the air
and twisting
oak tree branches

as if the arms
of the trees
weighed nothing
a feeling that there

is something
still inside
waiting to be discovered
a part of life

never yet realized
as if consciousness
is alight in the sun
showing all the darkness

in the deep forests
the wind taking hold
of your hand
showing you

the beautiful darkness
made by tree shadows
the things part of everyone
unseen

so peaceful
this cold day of gentle rain
singing birds silent

. . . . . . . . . . . . . . . .

this silence too
is like a repeated birdsong
overcast day

. . . . . . . . . . . . . . . .

shrouding the hills
in white waves of mystery
morning fog

. . . . . . . . . . . . . . . .

saddened by gray skies
sunshine climbs out
of my mind

# BLACK TRAIN

a black train comes chugging by
billowing white smoke

that wraps behind it like a white scarf
blowing in the wind

and the train curves around the hips
of a mountain dotted with fir trees

so huddled together that no sunlight
can touch the forest floor

and the lake on the other side
shines blue as the sky

a long line of light playing on the water
shining white as snow

showing where the sun points
with its hand of light

as the train makes its way around the bend
the sound of its chugging

dies down to a murmur
until the valley carries it

a whisper in the wind
softly the sound passes

in the wind and sun
until all that's left is

the silence of the mountain
and the memory of the black train

I am a seed
in the wind
searching
for a home.

. . . . . . . . . . . . . . . . . .

Life falls
so easily
in a storm.

I'm only visiting
before I melt
into the earth.

in a dark place
a flower rises
from dead leaves

. . . . . . . . . . . . . . . . .

October—
bare branches
whining like old doors

. . . . . . . . . . . . . . . .

a fallen leaf
crushes into the dust
of everything that falls

before flowers spring
from their sleep
        a silence falls
like the morning stillness
        under a soft sun

the cloud's shadow
moves so slowly
over the hills

rain pats the roof
as if a small animal
is running on it

. . . . . . . . . . . . . . . . .

the day is silent
but sunlight keeps on singing
in my heart

151

# THANK YOU

Thank you for reading my poetry book. I collect these poems for everyone's enjoyment.

If you don't mind, leaving a review would be greatly appreciated. Reviews help new people find my books. They are extremely helpful for an independent writer like myself, and I appreciate each one. You can leave a review on Goodreads or, if you bought this book from an online store, the store's website, or both.

In the meantime, before my next poetry book comes out in the following years, you can find me on social media sites. You can also email me at: lukelevi4@gmail.com
Instagram @lukelevipoet
Twitter @LukeLevi6

Goodreads: https://www.goodreads.com/lukelevi

# ABOUT THE AUTHOR

Luke Levi is a Texan poet. His poems can be found in *Humana Obscura, Presence, Akitsu Quarterly, Haiku Commentary, Autumn Moon Haiku Journal, Failed Haiku, Cold Moon Journal, Wales Haiku Journal, Trash Panda Haiku,* and elsewhere. You can often find him sitting outside, listening to birds singing in the Texas Hill Country.

Find him on Instagram @lukelevipoet and Twitter @LukeLevi6 and TikTok @lukelevipoet.

Printed in Great Britain
by Amazon

33186881R00096